PRAISE FOR RAYMOND B
& POLYGRAPHS AND PAPER CLIP BRACELETS

Boyd's investigative tales are as diverse as they are captivating. His ingenious methods for eliciting confessions showcase both his sharp wit and professional acumen. The breadth of cases he's cracked is truly remarkable.

—Ryan MacAfee

Vice President, Smile Brands

Boyd's expertise extends far beyond the polygraph. His unique approach involves building rapport with suspects, empathizing with their circumstances, and then skillfully extracting confessions. His track record of assisting countless businesses in rooting out dishonesty and theft is unparalleled.

—Bill Regan

President, Hirsch Pipe

Boyd's recounting of his criminal investigations is as authentic as it is engaging. His innovative confession-extraction methods, coupled with his quick wit, make for a compelling narrative. Each case leaves you eager for the next, showcasing Boyd's natural flair for storytelling, keen intellect, and remarkable recall. This book is a must-read for true crime enthusiasts.

—John Nerland

Former CEO, Mega Bank

POLYGRAPHS
AND
PAPER CLIP BRACELETS

RAYMOND BOYD

POLYGRAPHS AND PAPER CLIP BRACELETS

A PRIVATE INVESTIGATOR'S TOAST TO THE CRIMES THAT KEPT HIM THRIVING

Advantage | Books

Published by Advantage Books, Charleston, South Carolina.
An imprint of Advantage Media.

Printed in the United States of America.

10 9 8 7 6 5 4 3 2 1

ISBN: 979-8-89188-129-7 (Paperback)
ISBN: 979-8-89188-130-3 (eBook)

Library of Congress Control Number: 2024925050

Cover design by Matthew Morse.

07-21-2025 12:16

I was inspired to write my second book after losing my loving wife of sixty-seven years in 2022. Barbara was always a strong force behind my writing and encouraged me to share my stories of criminal activities. I knew I had many more stories to share after
God Bless Crime: It's Been Good to Me.

CONTENTS

PART I

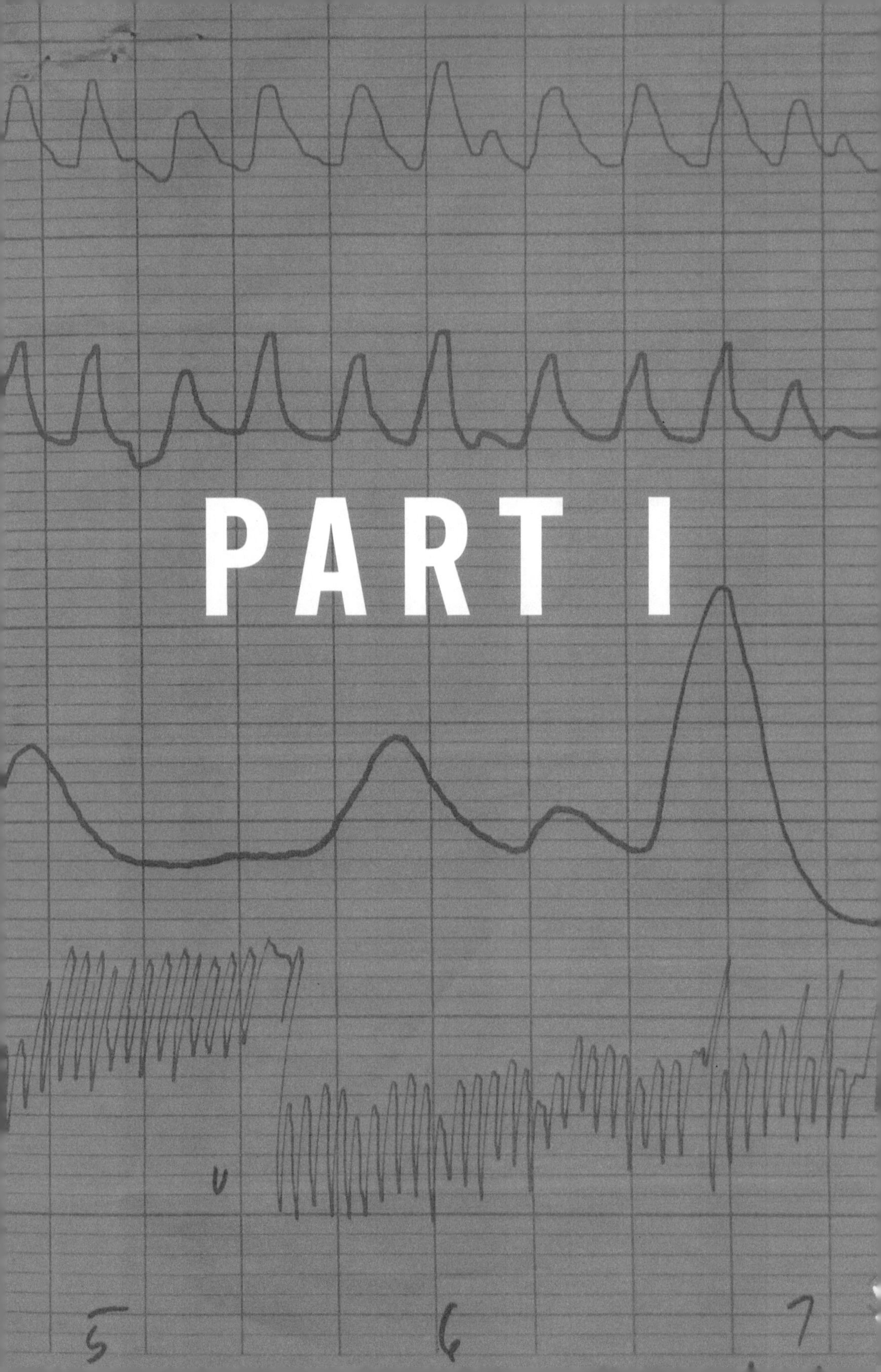

THE MAKING OF A DETECTIVE

WELL, FOLKS, you're about to embark on a journey through the early days of yours truly, Raymond Boyd. Fair warning: it involves military high jinks, stand-up comedy (and I use that term loosely), and more airline shenanigans than you can shake a stolen Polaroid camera at. You'll see how a young man with a knack for jokes and a nose for trouble stumbled his way into the world of investigations.

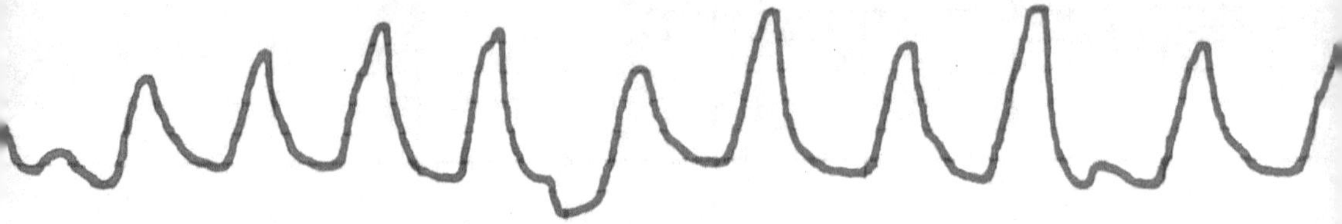

INTRODUCTION

AS I RELATED in my last book, *God Bless Crime: It's Been Good to Me*, I attended Fork Union Military Academy, a military high school in Virginia. A recent movie, *The Holdovers*, was about boys at a New England boarding school; the students were threatened with a transfer to Fork Union Military Academy if they did not behave. I begged my parents to send me there. It was good training and served me well.

I went on to college, working my way through the University of Massachusetts and Boston University as a stand-up comedian.

The question I get most about my career is regarding my work as a comedian. I told all the jokes I had stolen from television, plus a few more. I sang a song called "Wait for Me, Mary" and then told jokes about my supposed girlfriend, "Mary." They went like this:

She was so skinny she had to have suspenders to hold up her bra.

She was so skinny, I took her to a restaurant, and she was wearing a black dress. The waiter told me he had a rack for my umbrella.

She swallowed a grape, and two guys left town.

She ran for Miss America, and they almost pulled her citizenship.

The audience was not safe either—I started my act with "As I look into your faces, I realize there are some faces that need looking into …" Well, you get the picture. Jackie Gleason, I was not, but it got me through college.

While hanging out in a nightclub, I met a bunch of Boston cops. They recruited me to work for the Boston Police Department—my first, but not last, involvement with the police. I learned a lot, but the war was on as I graduated from college. Nobody, not even the police, was hiring men of draft age. So I entered the Army and got my training in undercover investigations. This set me on a career path I could have never imagined.

My love for jokes never died. My most successful one occurred after I left show business, and it was the joke that got me my first job.

The interviews for the director of security position at Capital Airlines had been long and tiresome. For the final effort, all five of the interviewing executives were present in the boardroom. One of the interview team members seemed to take a dislike to me and directed his most difficult questions at me. My caustic critic said, "Mr. Boyd, what investigative training from your service in the Army would be at all pertinent to the problems the airline might encounter? What makes you think you would be successful?"

My response broke up the room. I said, "Well, we won the war ..." My sponsor, the finance director, called me at home that evening. And he was still laughing when he told me I had the job and to report on Monday to start work.

The airline industry back in the 1950s was much different from today, and it offered me experiences and lessons I would keep throughout my career, some of which I've included in the following pages. The industry then and now seems like two different worlds!

I then went on to work for Globe International Detective System in Virginia. Globe sent me to California to open a West Coast branch. My wife, Barbara, and I arrived in California driving a convertible à la Lucy and Ricky, never to live in the cold of the East Coast again. Opening a brand-new office in California for Globe taught me everything I needed to know about running my own business.

On April 1, 1967, Barbara and I started our own company, Boyd & Associates. However, our most successful venture had to be our four kids: Jack (Ray Jr.), Kelly, Daniel, and Patrick.

Writing my first book was an interesting experience. I now have greater respect for writers who sit alone for hours composing. No wonder they drink so much! Despite the hard work, I enjoyed the process and felt I had more to share.

If you've read my first book, you might notice that this one has a different flavor. For *Polygraphs and Paperclip Bracelets*, I decided to take a more personal approach, with just a little editorial guidance. While *God Bless Crime: It's Been Good to Me* was a carefully crafted narrative of my adventures, this book is pure, unfiltered Ray Boyd. Maybe you'll think it's a bit rougher around the edges, sure, but it's also more intimate—like sitting down for a drink with me and hearing these stories straight from the horse's mouth. So if you're expecting the same style as the first book, well, you might be in for a surprise. But I hope you'll find that what this book lacks in literary prowess, it makes up for with authenticity and humor. After all, catching criminals isn't always a smooth business, and neither is writing about it!

In this book I get a little help from my friends. I hired a chief investigator, David Warkentine, who assisted me in some exciting adventures. The apple doesn't fall too far from the tree, and I also have some stories in which my kids do their own investigations , and my daughter assisted with the editing. I hope you enjoy the book as much as I enjoyed writing it!

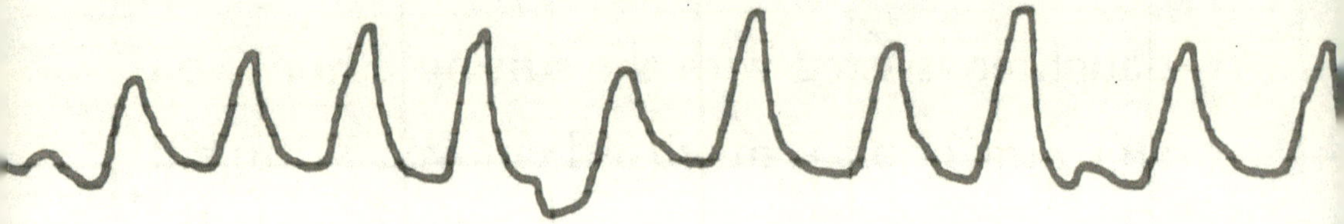

FURTHER ADVENTURES IN THE ARMY

APPARENTLY, SOLDIERS WITH top secret clearances were needed to witness the first test of a hydrogen bomb. I was the lucky member of our investigative team to be selected. A short flight from Travis Air Force Base in California and I was on my way to Enewetak in the Marshall Islands. We had a couple of days of "make-do work" Army style, and then the day for the big test was on. It seems the hydrogen bomb was to be the successor to the atomic bomb, only bigger and more destructive. As our coordinator lectured us, we were to blow up the Bikini Atoll some thirty miles away from Enewetak. All of us soldiers and witnesses were assembled on the beach and given some very thick sunglasses and a badge to measure the radiation, if there was any, from the bomb.

As soldiers will do when involved in a new dangerous situation, our jokes were flying thick and fast. We were ordered to kneel on the beach about ten yards from the water and instructed to keep our glasses on and wait for the explosion. The word "awesome" would do it an injustice. At first, it looked like a normal explosion, but then it spread left and right from our viewpoint. After that, it came rushing back to the center, and the island of Bikini came with it, palm trees and all. Our group of formerly joking witnesses was awestruck. Next, the great umbrella formed and towered over the landscape. No one was joking now. We all agreed that instead of making the whole operation secret, it should be publicized for the entire world to see. No one would let their leaders go to war ever again.

Barbara and I had just married. Our first child was conceived on the way home from the church. Seven years after that bomb test, we conceived our second child. Then children three and four arrived a year apart. Maybe we should have named those kids Radiation Two, Radiation Three, and Radiation Four.

However, my time in the Army wasn't all about high-profile missions and explosive tests. Sometimes, the most interesting intelligence came from the most mundane places. During one assignment I found myself working undercover as a bartender at a small local bar frequented by off-duty military personnel. It was there that I stumbled upon an unexpected bit of intel.

One quiet Sunday morning, with only my two regular customers in the bar, I overheard a conversation that piqued my interest. One of the two men, an Army dentist nearing discharge, was discussing his plans to steal equipment from his military office to stock his new civilian practice. As I pretended to wipe down the bar, I listened intently while he complained about the impossibility of smuggling out a dental chair. I gave the officer a free drink and from then on I owned him.

Their casual discussion of this planned theft was so brazen that I was tempted to say to them "Could you talk a little louder?" I had nearly dropped my pencil trying to catch every word! Instead, I kept my cool and reported the conversation to my handler. Within three days both men were unexpectedly transferred to Washington, DC. I later learned that the Criminal Investigation Division had taken over the case.

This experience reinforced a lesson I'd carry throughout my career: sometimes, the best intelligence comes not from elaborate sting operations but from simply keeping your ears open in the right places.

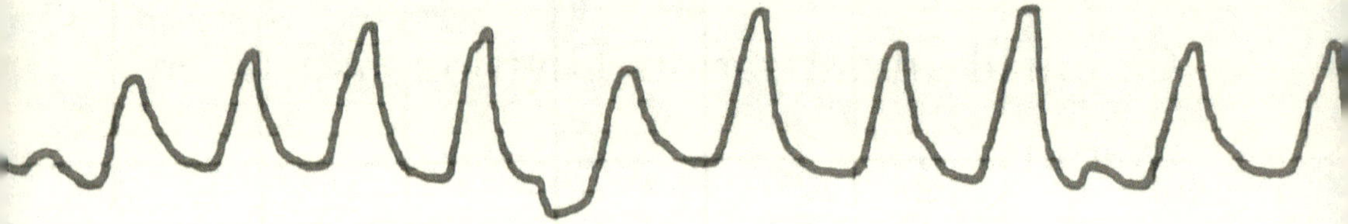

AIRLINE PERKS

FOR FIVE YEARS I served as director of security for Capital Airlines. At that time it was the seventh-largest domestic carrier in the United States. Just out of the Army, Barbara and I moved to a nice apartment in Arlington, Virginia. Driving to work on the George Washington Memorial Parkway each morning, I passed the Marine Memorial and the Pentagon. My office was located in a large building in the southernmost area of the very large property that comprised the Ronald Reagan Washington National Airport. The hangars for the maintenance center were on the ground floor and faced the airfield with a constant parading of aircraft in both directions. The corporate offices, including mine, were on the second floor.

In my earlier book, *God Bless Crime: It's Been Good to Me*, I related several interesting investigations I conducted. However, many of them were more humorous than criminal. While things have changed about law enforcement over the years, the fact remains that crime proliferates if it is not adequately dealt with. As the well-known theory says, a city that allows broken windows to remain will encourage more broken windows. The city that promptly fixes those broken windows will be much better off. Prosecuting little crimes leads to less crime.

While times change, human nature remains the same. Excessive drinking on airline flights has always been a bad idea that leads to bad results.

One of the strangest cases of this arose because the airline business is so wildly competitive. Capital Airlines and American Airlines had an all-out dogfight to become the preeminent carrier in the Washington, DC, to New York market. Security, scheduling, and giveaway perks all became weapons in the struggle, leading to several unusual incidents.

None was more entertaining than the elderly man who found flying to his liking because of his love of alcohol. Back then, alcohol was free on flights. This gentleman would buy a round-trip ticket from DC to LaGuardia. Naturally, they served liquor and other refreshments during the flight. When he arrived in New York, he would cash in his return ticket and spend the proceeds at the airport bar. He would then buy another ticket to Washington, DC; of course, the checks he used to purchase those tickets were bogus. (Try buying an airline ticket with a check now—you would be laughed out of the airport!)

Upon returning to DC, this gentleman would repeat his New York drinking extravaganza. Well, common sense would dictate that by his second or third trip, a savvy airline would get wise to the bad checks. However, it was not until the eighth trip that our revenue accounting office became suspicious and alerted security. (That would be me!)

When the next trip from New York to Washington was due to arrive, I met him at the gate, along with a police officer. I had already made a crime report for the bad checks. As the offender stepped off the plane, I read him his rights and turned him over to the District of Columbia police officer. The old gentleman's only comment was "Funny airline you work for, kid."

One of the airline's other great promotions consisted of new Polaroid cameras that our flight attendants used to take photos of the passengers and give them as keepsakes. I later learned that the airline had bought five cases of Polaroid cameras, with eight cameras in a case. In just six weeks, all the cameras were gone! What a waste of money.

My counterpart, Bill Smith—the director of security for Trans World Airlines—reminded me that Capital and Trans World Airlines had each been approved for a route to Florida from the Midwest cities. We decided on a bet to see who would be the first of us to catch a thief in Florida. I chose to concentrate my efforts on winning the bet by solving the case of the stolen Polaroid camera cases. There is a saying in police work: "A stoolie [a stoolie is someone who has previously been caught at a crime and is willing to work with law enforcement] will beat a fingerprint every time." Fortunately, I already had a stoolie in the Florida office of Capital Airlines.

I had previously caught a female ticket agent in New York stealing, but the amount of the theft was negligible. Apparently, this ticket agent had friends in high places, and a local politician became involved in the situation. This politician requested that the ticket agent simply be transferred to another office. I took it upon myself to be the face of the transfer, and despite my misgivings, I, too, spoke up for the former thief. Instead of being discharged, she remained employed and was transferred to Miami. Now she was my handpicked stoolie!

I called her. We met in a bar. The ticket agent was grateful for her continued employment and ready to unload all she had seen. She dutifully told me about all the thefts going on in the industry. At the time airline meals were becoming popular. Not just snacks such as peanuts, but full-on meals were served on the aircraft. She told me all about the employees in their feeding frenzy. It was interesting, but I wanted to know about the Polaroids. My stoolie quickly gave up a suspect.

Miami was a new market for Capital Airlines at the time. Capital was desperate for employees in a tight labor market where they were the new kid on the block. This was how Herb Johnson came to be hired without any background check at all.

During a visit to Miami for Capital Airlines, I talked briefly with almost all the new hires there. I thought several of them looked like potential problems, including Johnson. Management ignored my concerns. They did not think security was much of a priority and sarcastically suggested that I stop chasing thieves and help with luggage handling. I thought, *Maybe I will, but first, I have to get Herb Johnson.*

A police record check revealed that Johnson had been arrested for receiving stolen property. Further checking revealed he was on probation for that offense. The rest of his police record was sealed because of his age.

When I called Johnson in for an interview, we talked for a while about the Major League Baseball season, and he warmed up nicely. I then explained that I had researched his police record, but I did not want to be responsible for firing a good employee when we needed folks like him so badly. I suggested we explore his arrest and conviction. He became flippant and disrespectful.

I explained that, as a substitute for the background checks that management had neglected to do because of the rush to start Capital's Cleveland-to-Miami service, we were instead having everyone sign search consent agreements for their homes and cars. My stoolie had told me that Johnson hid the two cameras he got away with in his vehicle. I then explained that Capital made extensive use of hidden planted cameras, and I told him we had pictures of him putting the cameras in the trunk of his car. (This was not true, but Johnson did not know that.) With the consent form signed, we walked out to Johnson's car, and sure enough, two Polaroids were in the trunk.

I then said, "Considering your police record, and since you're a fellow baseball fan, how about we just lay you off?" Johnson wisely chose to be laid off. Sure enough, my stoolie was right, and the Polaroid thief was caught. It pays to have friends in low places. Bill graciously paid off our bet.

Even though I lacked business experience, I realized Capital was being managed like a candy store. One month, the airline magically showed a small profit, and what did they do? They used the profit to buy all new furniture for their office lobby. I had recently been on vacation with my wife and in-laws. I discovered my father-in-law's *Wall Street Journal* and read it cover to cover. I began developing an interest in business with a keen focus on management and management style.

One of the duties necessary in my line of work was the selection, training, and scheduling of security guards and investigators, including people who would work undercover.

I soon built a reputation among airline security people for choosing experienced and intelligent candidates for undercover jobs. I won't forget a friend of mine who worked for a very large transcontinental airline. At his request I sent him a female undercover operative, Arlene, who had recently done an excellent job unearthing a complicated insurance scam. He called me a few days later to tell me that Arlene was a lesbian. "How on earth did you ever come up with that?" I queried. My client quickly responded, "I asked her to go to bed with me, and she said no."

While I was at Capital Airlines, one of the employees was taking bets and acting as a bookie. The bookie went around soliciting bets, which seemed fun at first. However, soon, some employees experienced serious losses and became deeply in debt. The bookie's collector beat up one employee. This instantly came to my attention.

I broke the taillight of the bookie's car. I then called some friends at the local police department to report the vehicle with the broken taillight. The police pulled the car over and found betting slips in the passenger seat. That was enough to get the bookie fired.

My time with Capital Airlines was well spent. In addition to the investigations, which, of course, took priority, I was also attacking other security exposures that Capital management had completely ignored.

Anyone could walk into the Capital Airlines office building and go completely unchallenged. And more than half of the offices were left unlocked day and night. I first hired a security guard and placed him on duty at the main entrance to the building to screen the entrance. It would be months before I could issue badges and identification cards. I started a nighttime "lock your doors" program. I would go to the office personally and leave "courtesy tickets" at unlocked offices. One executive complained that the company was becoming almost prisonlike. My courtesy tickets graduated into strong memos. It was not until my memos were copied and forwarded to top management that I really felt some semblance of order was reached. At the same time, I instituted a security guard program. One officer manned the desk at the main entrance with radio contact available between himself and a second officer who covered varied routes within the boundaries of the property.

Finally, after almost a year of effort, we had a security program that would help keep honest people honest and expose those who had other interests. I decided to expand my efforts to ascertain that there was not the same careless handling of monies that I had witnessed in other functions within the company.

It was a lovely, warm day in October when I locked up my office and headed out for the approximately half-mile walk to the building that contained not only Capital's revenue accounting offices but also several other offices representing a myriad of related businesses. Ariel Schmidt, a short, smart-looking thirty-five-year-old woman, greeted me. Ariel had been with Capital for three years. Her boss was the vice president for finance and was headquartered in the same building, which was half a mile away from me. When I asked Ariel how often she saw her boss, she replied, "A couple of times a year." My interest was piqued.

When we got to Ariel's office, her boss went into a monologue about how little opportunity there would be for theft from his department. At my request Ariel took me through the journey that the typical airline ticket made, from the passenger to revenue accounting or the bank. I asked about possible exceptions. I quickly decided I needed more training—and from someone other than Ariel. My informant was a twenty-year veteran of the ticket counter minutia, who convinced me that someone was stealing, taking, or otherwise misdirecting the cash that came into the revenue accounting office. My informant told me exactly where to look. When I returned to Ariel, she was a frightened, blubbering piece of putty. I took her confession of stealing $86,000 and her resignation.

In 1957 I was elected chairman of the Airline Security Officers Conference. In May the security directors of every airline in the world attended the annual meeting at the Taft Hotel in New York.

Many items were discussed, and problems were shared. Passengers were becoming all too happy to order and consume alcoholic drinks during flights. Of greater concern was a frightening new problem: some fringe extremist groups were attempting to hijack airlines. This problem got the direct attention of our membership.

May 1, 1961, saw the first US airline hijacked to Cuba. A National Airlines Convair

440 flight from Marathon, Florida, to Key West was hijacked by a man carrying a knife and a gun. For several hours, air traffic authorities believed the flight was lost at sea. The aircraft landed safely, and the perpetrator was arrested.

July 31, 1961, was the first attempted hijacking of an airline on American soil. The incident was said to be inspired by numerous airliner hijackings from other countries to Cuba. A pipeline worker boarded and then attempted to overtake a Pacific Airlines flight at the Chico Municipal Airport in Chico, California, intending to return to his hometown of Smackover, Arkansas. He ultimately failed, but not before he shot two airline employees, blinding one for life.

The event that really brought hijacking to the forefront was Eastern Air Lines Shuttle Flight 1320. The plane was carrying passengers from Newark to Boston when it was hijacked around 7:30 p.m. The hijacker was armed with a .38-caliber revolver. He shot the copilot and then turned the gun on the pilot, a former United States Air Force pilot who had been promoted to captain six months earlier. The pilot was shot in the arm, and the hijacker attempted to force a crash landing. The copilot was able to force the gun from the hijacker's hand and shot him three times before collapsing into unconsciousness because of his own injury.

Despite having a .38 slug in his arm and bleeding profusely, the captain was able to safely land the plane at Logan International Airport. While communicating with air traffic control, the captain reported his copilot had been shot (but not himself) and requested an ambulance. Unfortunately, the copilot later died from his injury. The hijacker was arrested and hung himself while in jail awaiting trial.

At least a dozen attempted hijackings were recorded for the year 1961. Even though I was not directly involved in hijack prevention, I noted my mail was increasingly directed to the issue because it was already a frequent occurrence in other countries. My experience at Capital Airlines told me it was coming closer to home, fast. A joint effort by all the Airline Security Officers was proposed. We all composed letters. My letter to my boss at Capital Airlines went like this:

To: O'Ferrel Estes,

Increasingly, we are seeing hijacking and attempts at hijacking commercial airliners around the world. The Airline Security Officers believe security efforts should be enhanced before another attack is possible. This group strongly suggests a full security survey of all current procedures. One immediate suggestion would be to send all passengers through a metal detector before boarding. Also, after all boarding is complete, the door to the cockpit should be locked and secured and not operable until the flight is completed. I will certainly make myself available to assist with any implementation of the suggestions and any request for a full security survey.

RAYMOND G. BOYD

Fortunately, I did not have to concern myself with hijackers for too much longer because in 1961 I was recruited by an executive search firm to move to California to be the manager of a private investigation firm. I jumped on the opportunity. Luckily for me I did because in 1962 United Airlines took over Capital Airlines. My wife and I were on our way to California.

PART II

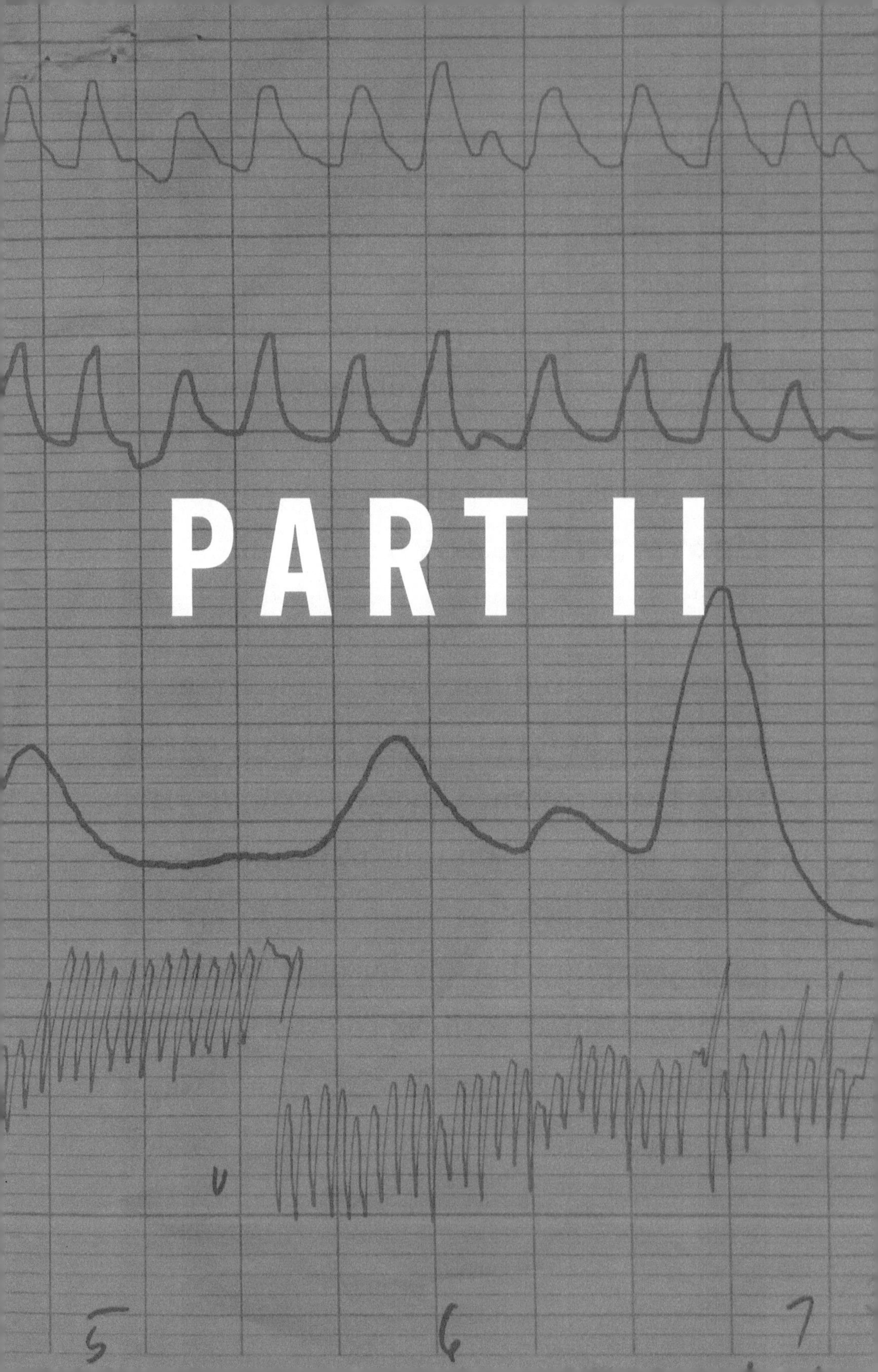

CASES AND CAPERS

WELCOME TO THE meat and potatoes of my career—or should I say the steak and scotch? In this section you'll get a front-row seat to some of my most memorable cases. From outsmarting not-so-clever criminals to chasing "wee people" with paper clip bracelets, these stories will show you that sometimes, the truth is stranger (and funnier) than fiction. Many times, our investigation would point to more security problems within the company that would inevitably lead us to supply the burglar alarm, closed-circuit television, fire alarm systems, and undercover investigations as needed. You'll learn all about these different security methods and might even pick up a trick or two for your next poker game—just don't tell 'em where you learned it!

CRIMINALS MAKE IT EASY

IF YOU READ my earlier book, *God Bless Crime: It's Been Good to Me*, you might have been struck by the number of cases that were solved not by the genius of the investigator but rather by the rank stupidity of the perpetrator. Many times, when the public reads about a complicated investigation resulting in an arrest, the average Joe might remark, "What a shame. If that thief had turned his same efforts into a legitimate pursuit, he could be very wealthy." I think this book will disabuse you of that conclusion. The thieves I have dealt with are typically so hard up that they must steal just to break even.

I think the most relevant facts were best summed up by a television episode of *Columbo* featuring Peter Falk as a Los Angeles police detective. A woman had been murdered, and Columbo suspected her husband (of course). The husband was a rather supercilious professor at the local college. As Columbo stumbled around in conducting the investigation, the professor chided him by remarking that he had not killed his wife, but if he had, Columbo was not smart enough to catch him. Columbo's response was classic: "Well, if you are like most people I investigate, you only commit one murder in your lifetime. I conduct these investigations every day of my working career. By now the odds are so heavy in my favor, and I have seen these crimes so many times and by so many people that catching you is a foregone conclusion."

There are many other examples of how criminals catch themselves. One story I heard, which the Boston police department was fond of regaling from time to time, was about a suspect in a rape case. While the suspect was slightly drunk, he was walked into the lineup room before the curtain was drawn. Accidentally, and in full view of a female victim, the suspect turned to the escorting detective and remarked, "Yep, that's her, all right."

There was also a veteran female detective in the Los Angeles police department who was arrested for the murder of her rival in a love triangle. How did she get caught, despite her obvious knowledge of police procedures? While investigating the original crime scene, officers found a used coffee cup from Starbucks. They obtained DNA from it. When other evidence cast suspicion on the female department member, detectives followed her to Starbucks one morning. Upon finishing her morning cup of coffee, she casually tossed her cup in an available trash can. The two trailing detectives retrieved the cup, and the subsequent DNA was a perfect match to the DNA on the cup found at the crime scene. When confronted with the incontrovertible evidence, the suspect confessed.

Here's another example. A guy murders his wife and takes her to a remote spot in the woods to bury her. After the deed, he calls his girlfriend from that very spot. Oops! Wrong move. Detectives research his phone records and determine what tower the call bounced off and where his location was to determine his whereabouts. The body of the deceased wife is promptly found.

Other behaviors that foil suspects are trust, or lack of it. Two culprits are separated, and one is certain he will not confess, but he is not so sure about his partner. Frequently, one of the suspects confesses and names his partner. Why do they confess? In many cases, these confessions are gained by undercover agents, and for the perps, part of the compulsion to confess is tied to wanting to earn some respect from the people with whom they may one day be incarcerated.

At times, I think that television will eventually expose all investigative techniques, and the criminals will catch on and get better at evading capture. When properly executed, however, the oldest investigative approach—the good cop/bad cop routine—can still get remarkable results, especially if done with proper authority by a reasonably good actor.

Everyone has become aware of the good cop/bad cop routine. I recall an investigation I conducted with the late John Faughnan. John was a big man with an impressive shock of gray hair. A retired New York City detective, he was a kindly man who thoroughly looked the part of everyone's favorite uncle.

In retirement, John was the director of security for a large national company. He and I were trying to solve a sizable embezzlement from John's employer. After much surveillance and record checking, we fixed our suspicions on a thirty-five-year-old shipping superintendent, Jackson Grimaldi, who had only been with the company briefly. Our suspect was the typical New York street thug. Investigators are frequently bewildered by how some people make it through supposedly sophisticated screening processes, and John and I were dumbfounded as to how this shipping supervisor ever got hired. He had an extensive police record for petty theft, and his credit was abysmal.

We decided to conduct our interrogation in my hotel room. We began with easy questions about his previous arrests, former employers, current family situation, and his knowledge of losses from his department. Our suspect's attitude was one of feigned indifference. It was noticeable that almost from the beginning of our session, Jackson directed all his answers to John, completely ignoring me. This irritated me, so I returned the questioning to Jackson's police record. I suspected he had not been entirely truthful in his first answers.

At this point, I had several options I could choose from to draw him out. I could smile and softly say, "It's going to be lonesome in heaven with just you and George Washington." Or if I wanted to get aggressive, I could come back with "You're a lying piece of shit, and I can prove it." Guess which option I went with. To really sell it, I stood up menacingly.

John, playing his part, pushed me aside and told me to go outside and cool off. I dropped a few bad words as I headed out the door.

As soon as I was safely out of the way, John moved closer to the suspect and explained that I was a hothead with a reputation for insisting on prosecution. He told him I did not have a very nice attitude toward people like him. John continued with a statement that their company loves Boyd, and therefore, I would probably be back shortly.

In his most grandfatherly manner, John kindly suggested that it would be better for Jackson if he handled this matter. He then went into a couple of clearing lines, attempting to clean this matter up with a frank admission.

John and I have used a variation of this approach on many occasions. I only worried about this approach once, when a suspect stood and looked as if he were intent on killing me. During that incident, John reacted slower than I would have liked. I asked John to play his role a little earlier in the future so I would not get killed!

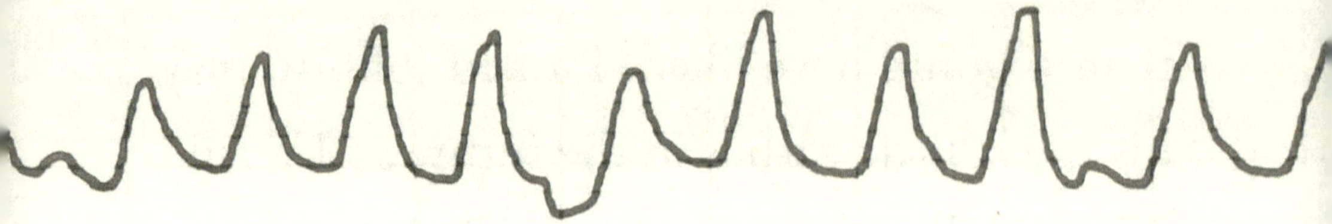

A SWANKY HOTEL

ONE MEMORABLE CASE involved the cocktail lounge at a very swanky hotel in downtown Washington, DC.

The client's complaint centered around a drop in revenue from the bar but no commensurate decrease in the liquor coming out of the storeroom—a common problem at bars and restaurants. I assembled three of my coworkers, and each of us brought our wives.

We had a round of drinks, and I was presented with the bill, which I promptly paid in cash. I left the paper bill with my payment.

The next couple offered to pay for the next round of drinks. The bill for the second round was the same one that had been presented to me for the first round. Again, the bill was paid with cash and left with the bartender. The same bill came around again for the third round.

So the bartender sold three rounds of drinks but only rang the sale up once. This meant that each time the waitress collected money for a round of drinks, she received, let us say, $100. After putting that first $100 in the cash register, the cocktail waitress and the bartender got to split the next two rounds of drinks between them. When I saw the next two rounds had not been rung up in the cash register, I excused myself and went to get the manager. The manager was waiting upstairs for this result, which we had predicted. I did notice that a couple of our ladies were affected by the drinks. They took their supporting role as the boisterous partygoers seriously and did their part to keep up the pretense.

The manager asked us to interrogate the two employees. I took the bartender to a vacant office, and my coworker took the waitress to another vacant room. We had previously marked the cash we used to pay for the drinks. Not surprisingly, the bartender had all our marked money in his pocket. The bartender confessed quickly. This bartender had a personality that could give good intentions a bad name. The waitress was a bit gutsier and held out for about an hour. She only confessed after assurances from me that her children would never find out why she "quit" her job.

They both confessed to taking a total of $15,000 each over time. The manager terminated them on the spot and thanked us for our work. Our wives did not thank us for including them in the investigation when they woke up the next day with hangovers.

This incident endeared me to my employer, the Globe International Detective System. The branch I was hired into prospered from day one. I was soon promoted to manager of seven regional offices in the Western United States. Following the business trend of the day, Globe soon went public and sold stock on the stock exchange. Because of my stock options, Barbara and I, along with our four children, moved to a very large home on a golf course in Granada Hills, California.

MISCOUNTING COINS

PERHAPS OPPORTUNITY is a large motivator for a thief. We certainly had a great number of clients in the coin-operated business, and one day my office received an emergency call. One of these coin-operated businesses reported that their gross collections had dropped significantly over the past two months. I took a tour of their building and saw a giant hole for theft. While they had two cameras in the collection room, there were several places where the workers could be out of the view of the cameras. Our client was so desperate for a quick solution that he implored me to launch an investigation immediately. "You know, with that lie detector box of yours, you have had many successful investigations in the past!" he exclaimed.

While my inclination was to do a thorough workup investigation before the polygraph, I confined my efforts to a police record check on the two employees who counted the coins. One of the suspects had a drunk driving arrest. That would be Louie. There was no record on the second, Jose. So based on the meager information from background checks, I decided on a slightly different approach to placate my highly nervous client. I worked out a plan with my partner. We noticed two small conference rooms. Each had a window in the door, so with minimal effort, you could see what was taking place inside the room.

I brought in the first coin counter, Jose, who looked like he might break first. I sat him in one of the conference rooms and told him to write out his job description, explaining what his duties were for the company. This took about fifteen minutes of instruction and cajoling. I obviously was not working with a brain surgeon. I asked him to proceed with my request to write his job description in his own words, and then I left him and said I would be back soon.

Next, I went to see my partner for that day, David, and Louie, the other suspect employee, in the second conference room. I instructed David to ask Louie whom he suspected in our recent loss of coins. Louie stated it had to be one of the bosses because they could come and go at will. David asked the standard questions and gathered information, such as Louie's full name, date of birth, current address, whether he had ever been arrested, married, children, birthplace, etc.

After some preliminary questions, we got to the hard questions. I told him, "I am investigating borrowing from the company and want to know the most you have ever borrowed in a day. You know we have cameras in the counting room, and last week, we had another camera hidden in another location, so do not add lying to your other untruths. I know you have a drunk driving arrest. Did you put that on your application here?"

My partner asked Louie questions for at least a half hour. In the meantime, I went back to my subject and told him about the polygraph test we intended to give him. I got him back to writing his job description, and my partner and his subject, Louie, now came to the door window where Jose was writing.

David told Louie that Jose was writing his confession, which implicated him.

Jose, at my behest, started writing out his thefts and admission to borrowings. David told Jose, "Louie says you showed him how to steal by going behind the partition before you seal the bags."

Jose readily admitted to taking money but said, "I did not take as much as Louie." We asked, "What is the most money you have ever taken in one day?" We professed displeasure at the first number he gave us and alluded to a far greater amount. We explained that our numbers were based on our forensic investigation thus far.

We took the most money stolen in a day, a daily average, and then we multiplied by when they started. It was always good to prompt them with something such as "Probably near Christmas that year." It was also an excellent time to remind them that this company did not give Christmas bonuses. Or "I bet you had to spend money for your grandmother's medicine." In short, we gave them an excuse and blamed the company for their behavior.

We explained their total number was based on the daily average of money stolen multiplied by the number of days they had worked. Jose and Louie agreed with our calculations.

We then handcuffed both men and took them out to Jose's vehicle. We found about $30,000 worth of Western Union receipts indicating they had sent the stolen money to Mexico.

Next, we contacted the Los Angeles Police, and two officers arrived and were given the signed confessions, the Western Union receipts, and all the evidence we had booked. One of the young officers objected to us having handcuffed the suspects. I said, "I am seventy-five years old, and this guy is twenty-five." I did not want to lose a foot race or get into a wrestling match with him.

The rookie cop looked at his sergeant, who said, "Tough to disagree with that logic." Our client insisted that a crime report had been filed and demanded a quick arrest. The police officers agreed and took custody of our two "perps."

Our prisoners were then locked up in the Los Angeles Wilshire Division and, at trial, given two years in jail and probation. Many times, in cases like this, the court will not only specify a jail term but will also insist on restitution as a condition of parole or probation. I later played golf with the client, and he chided me because I lost and had to pay him $30. He jokingly said I didn't have to pay if I didn't want to because the courts had been sending him $321 each month. When we caught the thief, the judge ordered restitution as a condition of probation. The monthly $321 was the amount the former employee had to submit to the court to stay out of jail.

FERTILIZER SHORTAGE

A SIZABLE AGRICULTURAL supply company called on Boyd & Associates to research losses they were suffering from their warehouse.

I first interviewed all members of the firm's top management, and they were all mystified by the randomness of the product shortages. I then set up an overnight weekend surveillance. No luck. The premises were locked up Friday at 5:00 p.m. They were open on Saturday for about four hours to accommodate their agricultural clientele. They were closed on Sundays.

The losses persisted, so we stepped up scrutiny of normal traffic, which seemed well accounted for by the work orders. The product that seemed to be most notably shorted at inventory time was an insecticide called Syngenta, which is used as fertilizer.

We decided to complete police criminal record checks on the entire workforce. A couple of the folks had a small record, but we did not observe anyone who had been culpable in any serious crimes. Sometimes, in this business, it is better to go back to the beginning and retrace your steps. The only clue we had was the theft of Syngenta specifically.

When I learned that Syngenta cost $800 per quart, my breathing raced a bit. It only intensified when I discovered why it was likely being stolen—the marijuana farmers who worked in the hills outside of Los Angeles appreciated the job that Syngenta did for their pot crops. Now came the hard part: catching the culprit.

I decided to take a long, hard look at the warehouse again. There were two entrances, one on each side, and both doors were wide open during business hours. It was a warm day in August, and I suspected they were open for ventilation. When I walked inside, the boss, Mr. Street, showed me where the Syngenta was stored.

Frankly, the building looked like a firetrap to me. The scrap lumber from discarded palates was stacked up everywhere. Now I had an idea! I shared my thoughts with my staff in the company. A knowledgeable group of folks handled the alarm business at Boyd & Associates, and I asked them first if my off-the-wall idea was feasible. I noticed the more in-depth we discussed the plan, the more enthusiastic the staff became. We had decided to place one of those ubiquitous red fire Exit signs over each door and configure them so closed-circuit television cameras could be serendipitously secured in each one. Our client agreed to have a skeleton crew work on the other side of the property on Sunday while my alarm crew accomplished the camera installation. We had three cameras in each dummy Exit sign. I would like to report that the installation went off without a hitch, but that wasn't the case. We had to return the following Sunday to make some adjustments to the aim and function of the cameras.

Our effort was not all in vain, though. Thanks to the hidden cameras, we had identified a suspect. Fredrick seemed to spend more time than necessary in the area where the Syngenta was stored. He even moved about four bottles of the product to a spot closer to the exit for no apparent reason. I commenced a background investigation on Fredrick.

Fredrick had two prior arrests, and both were for narcotics offenses. He appeared to be a low-level drug seller, and that type is frequently the person called upon by the real dealers to be a "gofer." Gofers are usually people who are regular drug users and pay for their habit by running errands for the higher-level drug distributor.

The next day we reviewed the video captured on the hidden camera. I printed out a picture of Fredrick hanging around the area where the Syngenta was stored. When I interviewed him, I told Frederick, "I will bet your mother would love to have one of these pictures for the family album." He first made a weak denial. But the picture of him with two bottles of Syngenta in his arms while exiting the building was sufficient to gain a weak agreement from him.

We spoke for about a half hour on unrelated subjects and then returned to the topic of

Syngenta. Finally, Fredrick admitted to stealing several bottles of the product. However, he would not give up any of his associates.

Finally, I told him to stand up and put his hands behind his back. He acted like he was going to make trouble. Fortunately, he complied. I asked the receptionist to call the local police department and ask for someone to transport a prisoner. I had Fredrick handcuffed and waiting for the two officers who responded.

Fredrick admitted to stealing about fifty bottles of Syngenta and later went on trial. He was a thoughtful guy who eventually felt he could arrange a better deal for himself by handing up another group of thieves. Accordingly, I met with Fredrick at a local coffee shop, where he named everyone he could think of at the company as participating thieves. I selected the three individuals he named as the most egregious thieves and then got these men to agree to a polygraph test.

It was a relief to management when all three men passed their polygraph tests and were certainly not guilty of theft. Throughout this entire ordeal, Fredrick would not give up the person to whom he sold the fertilizer. He was sentenced to six months in jail and required to pay my client restitution as a condition of his probation.

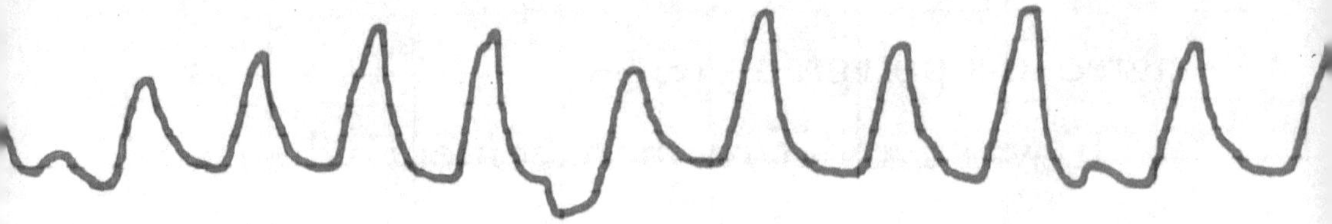

THE "JIG" IS UP

ANOTHER INTERESTING assignment for Boyd & Associates was with a manufacturing plant in Santa Ana, California, that produced various outdoor furniture using expensive aluminum jigs.

A jig is a prototype of a product that will be presented to a potential customer. It can be produced in any volume. Sometimes, jigs may be manufactured in steel, wood, plaster, brass, copper, or, in this case, aluminum. The company had invested a lot of research and development in these jigs.

They stored the jigs outside under a lean-to-type structure along the side of their plant wall in a fenced storage yard. The only security they had outside was a chain-link fence and a cinder block wall along part of the south wall of the yard.

The plant was experiencing "mysterious disappearances" of these jigs, valued at anywhere from $15,000 to $25,000 and up. Boyd & Associates had done the alarm system for the company, but there were no surveillance cameras outside. They hired us to do a one-man surveillance over a long weekend. I asked our investigative manager, David Warkentine—whom you'll get to hear a story from in a later chapter in part 3—to handle the job, and because of its importance, he took a personal interest.

The following Friday and Saturday passed without any result, but then on Sunday I decided to stop by myself to keep David company. Shortly after I arrived on Sunday morning, David stopped our conversation, saying, "Shush … What is that?"

We looked up and saw a guy in his twenties climbing over the wall. David and I immediately started toward the wall, but our intruder had already landed on the ground and was preparing to throw a mean-looking set of bolt cutters at us. Fortunately, David pulled out his gun. He pointed it toward our new arrival while I took him to the ground and handcuffed him.

We had previously alerted the Santa Ana police of our stakeout and called them to meet us. Two officers arrived to pick up the suspect and his bolt cutters. As it turned out, the suspect had already grabbed an expensive jig and set it aside to come back for a little later. The Santa Ana police officers who responded took the suspect into custody and commented, "Nice job, Boyd." The suspect later confessed to police that he was responsible for all the prior thefts.

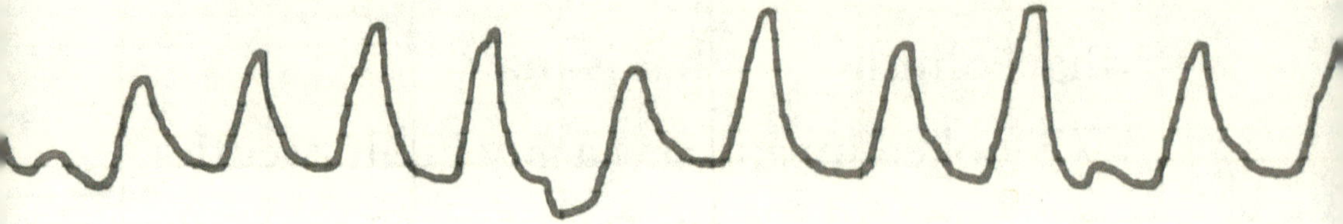

WHO DONE IT

ONE OF OUR BURGLAR alarm clients called to complain that he had suffered a loss of $25,000 from his briefcase that had been sitting unlocked on his desk all day. He did not discover the loss until he got home from work. By this time, everyone had left for the day, so I told him we would be in to see him at 9:00 a.m. the next day.

When we showed up, the client set us up in a small conference room and gave us a list of all employees who had access to the offices. We decided to give each employee a behavioral analysis interview. That is fancy talk for "Let's go ask people what they know about the crimes." The final question was "Do you have any objection to taking a polygraph examination?" When they agreed to the examination, I would have them sign a polygraph consent form, which I would always attach to my final report. Everything went fine, and I did not discover anyone I thought was culpable.

The last employee questioned was a very attractive and quite well-built woman. When she entered the room, she gave my partner, David, a warm handshake and a big hug. When David sat opposite her, she moved her chair so close they were practically knee to knee. David started to ask her the usual questions. She started with the company when she was eighteen and had held various jobs over the years. She was, at the time, in bookkeeping and shipping. By now she had her hand on his leg and was moving it up rapidly. With a big smile on her face and a "come hither" glance, she readily agreed to the polygraph.

She warmly shook his hand and gave him a big smile when she headed out the door. I thought I probably had my thief. However, she passed the polygraph with flying colors. We were nonplussed but could only continue the investigation and polygraph testing. David and I were very discouraged because we were out of suspects and had no reasonable alternate avenues of investigation to follow. David ended up leaving to work on another investigation, and while I packed up my equipment, the client stopped by to chat. As he and I talked, another middle-aged female approached us and expressed interest in my work, even going so far as to say "I would really like to take a lie detector test sometime."

Some inner motivator pushed me to blurt out "How about right now?" Her name was Maxine, and she was our client's daughter. She excitedly agreed, and we got right into the preliminaries. She asked what questions I would ask her and joked around, saying she would like to get her boyfriend on the polygraph. I drew up the questions and, of course, included questions about the money stolen from her father's office. She called the question unfair because her father had always encouraged her to come to him for money. I, in turn, had to encourage her to tell me if she took money from her dad on this occasion, and she immediately admitted to taking the $25,000 from her dad's briefcase the day before. She dismissed any concern because she said she was going to give him back what she hadn't spent already. When we told her dad, he hugged her and said it was all right.

It broke David's heart when I told him the thief was the client's daughter, who turned out to be a doper. She had helped herself to the $25,000 in cash to support her habit. The client paid me but did not say anything more about the loss of money.

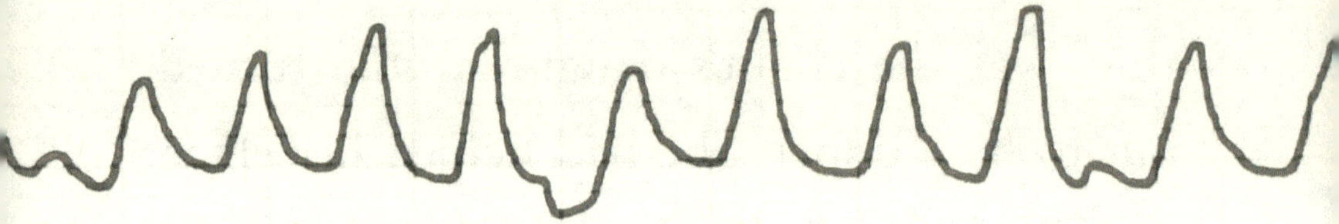

A THREAT TO KILL

EVERY EMPLOYER is wary of threats to clients, customers, and employees. This case concerns an employee who seemed intent on harming another. The client's human resources (HR) department became aware of one employee threatening another. The two employees were competing for the same supervisory position, and the acrimony between them was becoming problematic.

One of the employees (we will call him Jimmy) had threatened his rival with a death threat. The HR department investigated the situation and found credible evidence that a threat had been made, so they arranged to terminate Jimmy.

The HR person contacted the Boyd & Associates supervisory security officer assigned to the plant to escort Jimmy out of the office to his vehicle. They requested our investigation department surveil Jimmy for seventy-two hours to be certain he did not act on his threat to assault the employee who was the target of his jealousy. The Boyd & Associates investigation department, under the supervision of my partner, David, was prepared. As Jimmy was walked to his vehicle, our surveillance team stood by to start their job.

Once in his truck, Jimmy took off, and the chase began. The guy was a speed demon, and he left the client's parking lot at a high-speed rate in the direction of his residence. We knew where he was renting a room, but he lost my partner at a stop sign, so David just went to Jimmy's house and spotted his truck parked out in front.

Initially, it was easy surveillance. We had round-the-clock operatives watching him, and he only occasionally went to fast-food restaurants or convenience stores for meals. At one point, we followed Jimmy when he took off north on Highway 101 in the direction of Santa Barbara. He pulled off at a stretch of beach called the Rincon and just sat in his truck and stared out at the Pacific Ocean.

We discontinued our surveillance after seventy-two hours, as per our initial contract. We turned in our report, but the next day, we received an urgent call from the client informing us that Jimmy had brandished a twelve-gauge shotgun at his rival when they'd crossed paths in their vehicles near the client's plant.

We later learned that Jimmy was going to the plant to pick up his final check. The rival had flipped him off when he saw him on the road. Jimmy told us that he feared the rival was also going to ram him with his vehicle, so he pointed his unloaded shotgun at him to scare him off.

Upon receiving the report, we attempted to resume surveillance, but nobody knew where Jimmy had gone. We went to his residence and did not see his truck, and he had not been seen at the plant since the incident with the shotgun.

After driving around looking for him for several hours, we remembered the trip to the Rincon and decided to check that location. Sure enough, there was Jimmy, sitting in his truck bed and staring out at the ocean.

We took up a position about a quarter of a mile west of him in the broad parking area of the Rincon and called the client to tell him that we had located Jimmy and had him under surveillance.

The client advised us that a report had been filed with the Ventura County Sheriff's Office, and they would be passing along the location to the sheriff.

Soon after, we saw a California Highway Patrol vehicle coming up behind and to the left of us, so we flagged him down and pointed out Jimmy's location. The highway patrol officer held his position, and shortly thereafter, we could see the Ventura Sheriff's SWAT team taking up strategic positions on all sides of Jimmy, along with a Ventura Sheriff's helicopter that came into view and hovered over Jimmy while SWAT closed in on him.

Jimmy was taken into custody without incident. It was a Friday, so he was held in jail over the weekend and arraigned the following

Monday morning. He pled not guilty at his arraignment, and the court imposed a $2,000 bail bond. We were aware of the time and date he would be released and resumed surveillance. The bail bondsman picked him up and took him to the impound, where he paid for the towing and storage of his truck.

The bail bondsman noticed that we were surveilling them, pulled over to the side of the road, and flagged us down to ask why we were following them. We told him that Jimmy's previous employer hired us to do so.

It turned out that Jimmy had been evicted from the home where he was renting a room when he told them he had lost his job and could not pay in advance. So he planned to live out of his truck until he could find work. Jimmy was not a bad kid once you got to know him. I began to feel sorry for him. I was also concerned about keeping tabs on him.

I had a forty-four-foot sailboat at Peninsula Yacht Anchorage that needed some paint and varnish work, so I suggested he stay on the boat and do work in exchange for a place to stay and a small salary. He agreed.

During the period between his arraignment and preliminary hearing, we had several chats with Jimmy. It was clear to us that he was not quite "all there." He told us that now that he was not a scientist anymore, he planned to go back to his hometown of Valparaiso, Indiana, for a short time and become a porn star.

In one of these chats, he also told us that he and the alleged victim had been friends until this management position became available, but then his friend started spreading rumors about Jimmy to make him look like a less desirable candidate for the job.

At the time of the alleged weapon-brandishing incident, Jimmy was traveling to our client's building to collect his last paycheck when he saw his adversary driving in the opposite direction that he was traveling. The adversary flipped him off and swerved toward him across the center line. Jimmy told me us was merely signaling his intention to defend himself by pointing his unloaded shotgun toward him. We will never know whether this was the truth or not because both guys were "one brick short of a load."

(An interesting aside is the fact that about two years later this same client contacted Boyd & Associates, employing us to follow and surveil the victim—in this case, Jimmy's adversary—who had threatened a female supervisor at the plant. Following the victim around this time again took an investigator with race car driving skills because the suspect loved to drive at speeds more than ninety miles per hour in his Beamer sport coupe on the freeways of Southern California. The guy was followed to a motel holed up with a hooker just off the Pasadena Freeway in Glendale with easy access to several freeways. Now back to my story.)

We reported to the client that Jimmy was staying on a boat in the Channel Islands Harbor, figuring that would be the end of it, but it was not. The client returned to us and reported that their employees still feared retaliation from Jimmy since he was out on bail. Jimmy knew where all these employees lived, so the client authorized surveillance operatives to monitor their homes from the time they got off work until midnight or one o'clock to ensure their safety. So two investigators took twelve-hour shifts watching Jimmy.

At one point, Jimmy's old rival and victim decided he and several friends who were also former employees wanted to go out clubbing on a Friday night. When management learned of this plan, they wanted additional surveillance and executive protection for the victim and his buddies.

We quickly decided to have some off-duty Ventura sheriffs and Oxnard officers accompany them while they were out. At one point, one of the Oxnard officers mentioned that the victim and his friends appeared to be snorting cocaine and asked us what we wanted them to do about it. We said they should respond as they would with anyone else, but we never heard another word about it, and the client did not take any action with the employees that I know of, based on our report.

When Jimmy went back to court for his trial, he changed his plea on the advice of his public defender to guilty. He was sentenced to six months in county jail and five years of summary probation. He began his sentence forthwith and was whisked off to the Ventura County jail. David and I had Jimmy's truck and all his meager possessions from the boat. With Jimmy safe in jail, the surveillance and executive protection were discontinued. There was peace and harmony in Ventura County.

Ninety days later, Jimmy was released from jail, and David and I picked him up and took him out for breakfast at a local restaurant.

The client advised that they wanted us to resume round-the-clock surveillance of Jimmy for a period of two weeks, which we did, although we told them we did not think this was necessary.

We resumed our surveillance without incident except for the fact that during one of Jimmy's midnight runs to the doughnut shop around the corner from my boat, he was T-boned on the driver's side of his truck.

In an unrelated incident, our night shift investigator was hauled out of his van, handcuffed by local police, and held in the parking lot overlooking the boat while we were called to verify that he was there on business for us and not a vagrant.

At the end of two weeks, we followed Jimmy to a local salvage yard, where he sold his T-boned truck for parts. We then took him to the Los Angeles airport and put him on a flight back to Indiana. (Unfortunately, we have no idea if he succeeded in the pornographic industry!)

"WEE PEOPLE"

BEING LISTED IN the telephone book as a private detective frequently leads to some unwanted business. That is how I met Mrs. Murphy. It was a warm day in July, and I was thinking about sneaking away for a little round of golf. However, our long-suffering secretary, Eve Sorter, had another meeting in mind for me.

Apparently, Mrs. Murphy had come by and announced that she wanted to see the manager. Eve made an appointment for me to meet this lady the following afternoon. Now our clients are almost all exclusively corporations and reasonably large businesses. I thought perhaps Mrs. Murphy represented one of them. She was a reasonably attractive, well-dressed lady in her fifties. After she had been seated and given a glass of water, she began her story.

Beginning about a month earlier, she had noticed some unusual-looking people following her around. And they were tiny.

She said they were not always around but often enough to be disconcerting. She had reported this to her family, but they gave it no credence. When she persisted, her daughter suggested she make an appointment with her doctor.

By now I had decided Mrs. Murphy was the genuine article and not some actress my staff used to play a joke on me.

I worked with Mrs. Murphy for about half an hour. I am not certain I accomplished much, but we agreed when we looked at the roof of the adjoining building that the "wee people" were gone. I cleverly asked her if she was Irish. Reason being, the Irish believe in the "wee people." I know my family always did. My Irish mother would talk about them, and everything was blamed on them—the good, the bad, whatever.

Mrs. Murphy did not surface again for several weeks, and when she did, I was swamped. She waited patiently, and I tried to be kind, but I am sure I was less than accommodating. After she left, I decided that rather than having her return and waste my time, I would have to come up with something dramatic. And that was when it hit me!

About three weeks passed before Mrs. Sorter informed me Mrs. Murphy had come to visit again. I went to the waiting room and effusively greeted Mrs. Murphy, ushering her into my office. I then presented her with a bracelet, assuring her that it would chase the "wee people" away. I had made it myself, and she appeared genuinely excited as I strapped it on her wrist. It featured real paper clips!

Mrs. Murphy left my office as happy as I had seen her. She flashed her new paper clip "wee people" chasing bracelet for everyone in the office to see. As soon as Mrs. Murphy was out of sight, the office broke into gales of laughter. I, of course, basked in the center of my triumph. All went well until I arrived at the office on Monday morning.

A very loud, belligerent young man accosted me and said I was making a fool out of his mother and their entire family. My paper clip bracelet was the joke of their neighborhood. Mrs. Murphy's son claimed he had already contacted an attorney. In addition to the legal response, they planned to contact the state of California licensing authority to have me stripped of my investigative license. He intimated that the lawsuit would undoubtedly be in the six-figure area. My sincere apology did not appear to assuage any of the ire directed at me.

I explained to Mrs. Murphy's son that I never charged his mother for any of my advice, and the bracelet seemed to appease her and drive away the "wee people" from her mind—we hadn't heard from Mrs. Murphy since I gave her the bracelet. I kind of missed her. No lawsuit was ever filed, and I kept my license.

PART III

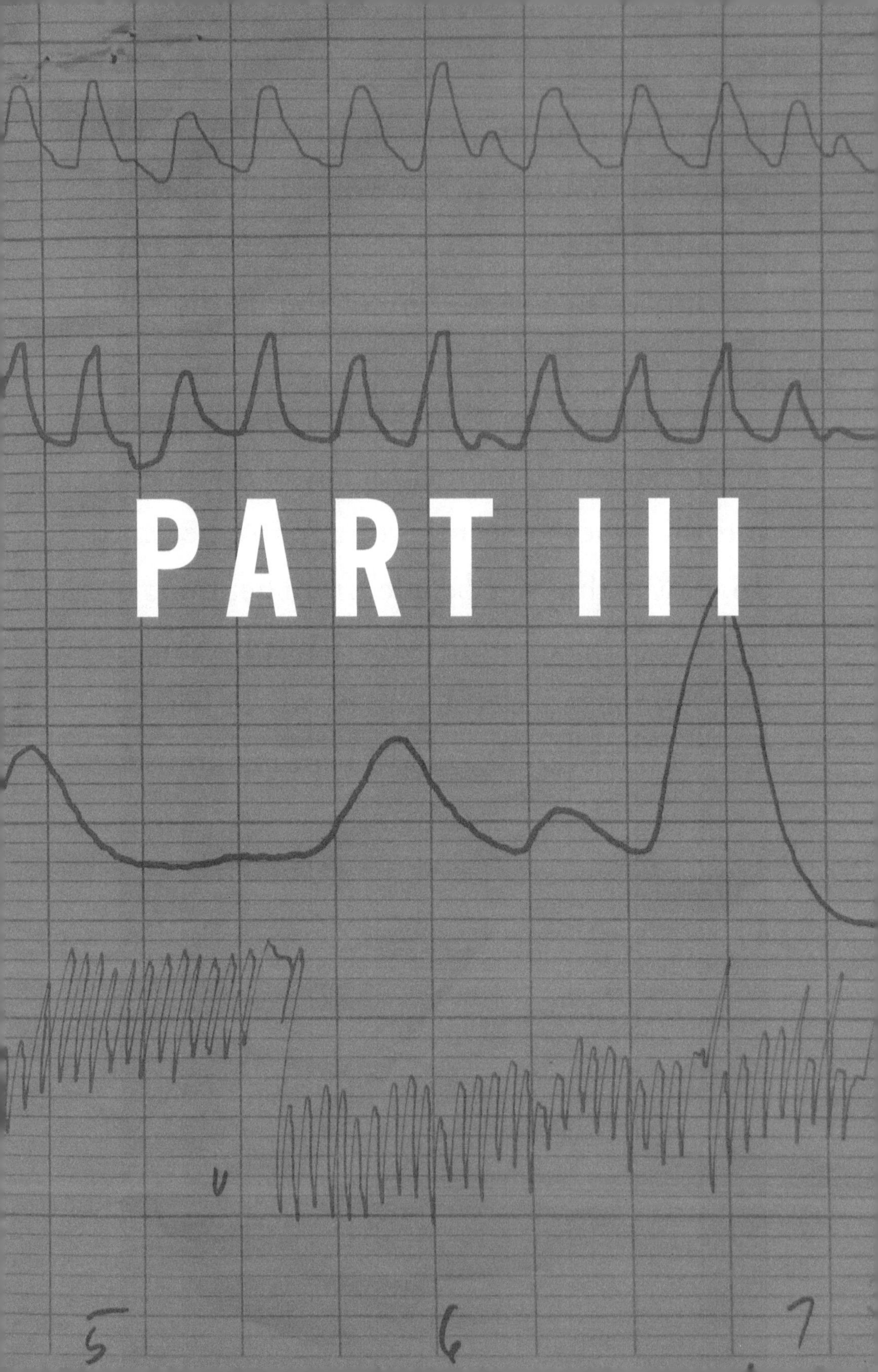

THE BOYD FAMILY BUSINESS

THEY SAY THE APPLE doesn't fall far from the tree, but in the Boyd family, it seems to roll right into the detective agency. In this part of the book, you'll hear a couple more stories from me, but more importantly, you'll get to hear stories from and about my kids as they share their own adventures in the family trade. From golf ball heists to wine capers, it turns out crime-solving is as much a part of our DNA as my receding hairline. You'll also get to hear a story involving our investigative manager, David Warkentine, who's been an extension of our family ever since he joined us at Boyd & Associates. So sit back, pour yourself a glass of "evidence" (wink, wink—you'll get it later), and enjoy these tales of the next generation of Boyd investigators. Just remember, in this family, what happens in the interrogation room … usually ends up in a book!

AROUND THE OFFICE

WE CERTAINLY HAD our share of strong characters in our company history. Our controller was a great guy named Andy Skarupa. Andy was the best kind of controller in that he was nothing if not cost obsessed. He was the kind of controller that if someone needed a new pad of paper, they had to give him the cardboard backing of the last pad. He counted every pen and pencil in the place. When Andy first came to us, the business was a mess. I was more interested in chasing thieves than running the business. Andy immediately took charge of the business end of things. We had a long list of overdue bills. Andy went to work on the list, and we had no debt after three months. He renegotiated all the debts downward and got everything paid and on track.

Andy was a pack-a-day smoker. Sometime in 1975 cigarette prices increased to an amount that Andy could not justify paying anymore. When Andy got down to the last cigarette in the last pack he would ever buy, rather than smoke it, he put it in his top desk drawer and quit smoking cold turkey. He kept that one cigarette in his desk drawer and looked at it every day to remind him not to smoke. The best part was that now that Andy had stopped smoking, he insisted everyone not smoke. Two employees who enjoyed smoking objected. They marched into Andy's office and said it was their God-given right to smoke. Andy declared himself to be God inside the Boyd & Associates building. One of the employees quit, but the one who stayed stopped smoking. Pretty soon, Boyd & Associates was smoke-free.

Andy had his quirks. Every day at 4:18 p.m., you could find him walking from his second-floor office down to the first-floor break room with one can of warm Budweiser in his hand. He would put the beer into the freezer, then he would walk back up the stairs. At exactly 5:00 p.m., he would return to the break room refrigerator and retrieve his beer, which was now chilled to the perfect temperature. Andy would drink his one beer at his desk and keep working late into the evening. He never had more than one beer. We waited for the day when Andy would get busy and the beer would freeze, but that day never came.

It was perhaps inevitable that my polygraph and investigation business would outstretch the labor-intensive security and patrol service.

Dan Boyd, my son, joined my team and immediately became a crack salesman. Dan is a first-class licensed polygrapher with a degree in business from Loyola Marymount University, which is his expertise. Specifically, he is an expert in the art of acquisition of small alarm companies. We have seen him acquire as many as nineteen businesses without hard feelings or lawsuits.

One day in the office, a loud bang that sounded like a gun went off. Dan took over, ran downstairs, and found a guard who had just returned from patrol. The guard was checking his gun, and the weapon was accidentally fired. The bullet went through the ceiling, traveled to the second floor, and lodged in the attic.

One of the Boyd & Associates competitors had an incident where the guard was checking a backyard when a pit bull came after him. The guard, thinking he was doing the logical thing, shot the dog. The lawsuit that followed that incident nearly broke that small firm. Dan immediately wished to eliminate the armed guards division of Boyd & Associates. But alas, the two businesses seemed to complement each other. I would conduct an investigation that would yield a confession and, on many occasions, an arrest. Boyd & Associates became the favored provider for any type of security the client could need, such as burglar, fire alarm, or secret shopper.

As our business continued to grow, we faced a significant challenge: finding qualified people to do the work. Police departments are generally understaffed, leaving business executives who suspect security issues with few options beyond filing a crime report. In the security business, the challenge begins with finding capable security guards, but it becomes even more difficult when searching for skilled investigators.

I've always enjoyed teaching, and at this time I was instructing interrogation one night per week at the Los Angeles Institute of Polygraph. I thought I might be able to recruit one of the graduates to join Boyd & Associates. I was particularly interested in David Warkentine, who was working as a bank investigator. To get a better look at him, I invited David to accompany me and our surveillance team on an operation one Friday night.

The case was typical: A carpet manufacturing company in downtown Los Angeles was suffering theft of finished product. An undercover investigator had observed the night foreman loading his personal truck with finished product during his four-to-twelve shift. This foreman was responsible for locking up the plant at the end of the shift. David and

I put together a surveillance crew and followed him one night after he'd clocked out as he drove home. The suspect rolled into a garage at a modest home in Van Nuys.

At the same time, one of our surveillance crew on foot reported back that the two-car garage appeared to be a resting place for a large stock of carpeting. Our suspect drove in, parked his truck, and walked back out through the garage before entering his house by the front door. That was when one of our most experienced investigators, John Liles, said, "Watch this," and broke into a run for the house.

I had seen this act before. There are three ways to make a lawful search: incident to an arrest, with a warrant, or with consent. Then of course, there's John Liles's method …

Reaching the front door, John banged hard. At 5'10" and 260 pounds, John was puffing pretty hard. When the suspect answered the door, he said, "What the hell do you guys want?" John, still out of breath, huffed, "There's smoke coming out of your garage." Brushing us all aside, the suspect ran to the garage door and opened it, revealing the stolen product inside. All I had to say was "You have the right to remain silent, but you're under arrest—all that carpeting is stolen property."

After that, the only thing David Warkentine could say was "You guys are great. I want to join your team." And that was how we got David. In the next chapter, you'll read about the missing heiress, a case that David treated as if his own daughter were the victim. I asked David to write his report on the heiress to incorporate the story into this book. The writing that follows is all David Warkentine's work.

THE MISSING HEIRESS

By David Warkentine, Investigative Manager

I FIRST MET RAY BOYD while attending polygraph school at the Los Angeles Institute of Polygraph. He was the interrogation lecturer. At the time I was a "special" in the audit department of a major West Coast bank. My job took me all over the state, investigating conflicts of interest, major "kites," and mysterious disappearances of money. I did many interviews and interrogations, which dovetailed into

Ray's investigation and polygraph work at his company, Boyd & Associates.

Attending polygraph school with Ray as the instructor was a stroke of luck for me. He taught techniques that I could not have learned otherwise and gave me insights that would have taken me years to gain had I been on my own. I always looked forward to getting a call from Ray because I knew there would be something interesting to learn. Ray's motto was "God bless crime: it's been good to me."

One day Ray called me and recounted an urgent story. The teenaged daughter of a wealthy and well-known Hollywood producer had gotten in a fight with her mother and run away from her New York home. Ray assigned me to the case, and I started by interviewing the distraught father. He was frantic as he recounted his diatribe, informing me that his daughter, Naomi, had a penchant for the

Hollywood scene and had even been an extra in a couple of movies. She was believed to be living on the streets of Hollywood, California. I knew I had to get Naomi home. So I called a friend of mine.

Michael (whose name we've changed to protect the innocent) was a very streetwise man who lived in the heart of Hollywood. He had been helpful in a couple of cases before, so I reached out to him for assistance.

Michael asked for some recent photos of Naomi, which we provided. He had them printed and circulated throughout Hollywood through a network of "street urchins" and runaways living there at the time (and who probably still do). On the flyers we listed a small reward for information.

Michael knew he could get information from his sources with the right kind of reward. We had several nights of touring the seedy part of town, but Michael came through for us. Through some street contacts facilitated by Michael and a few well-placed payments to informants, we received a tip on Naomi's location. Our missing heiress was reportedly being held in a shabby residence on Orange Grove Street.

Ray brought our team, and we set up surveillance, watching the house for a couple of hours. Our surveillance revealed that there were probably only six people coming and going, and it appeared that no one used a key to enter. This was an easy break for our side.

Five of us entered the residence, and four more were outside for added protection. I announced in a loud voice that we were there to get Naomi. With no response, we started sweeping the house. The first bedroom door we opened revealed Naomi sitting and crying in front of a television set. She seemed to realize we were there to help her and came along without a problem.

We immediately headed for the Los Angeles airport, where we booked a room for her at the Holiday Inn. We had two female employees of Boyd & Associates stay with her. We called her folks in New York, who immediately arranged to come to California.

The two women we'd left with Naomi reported that she had told them a harrowing story about being raped repeatedly and her captors attempting to prostitute her. Her mother and father were effusive in their gratitude to the Boyd & Associates personnel involved in the recovery.

I was told the parents were forever grateful, but I never heard a word about how the daughter turned out. I am sure she was grateful as well, and I do hope she never tried to run away again.

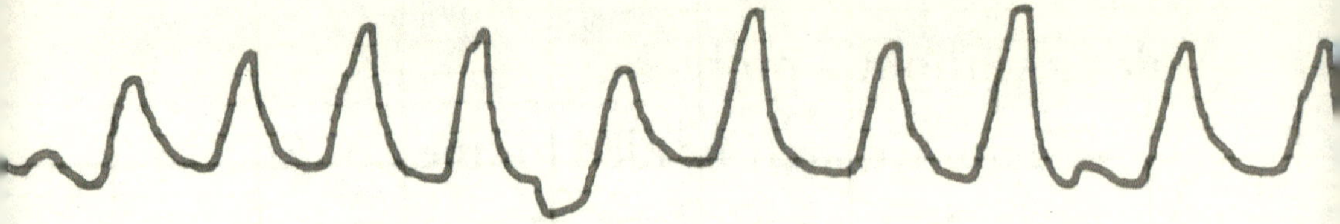

WHO STOLE MY BIKE?

MY SON DAN was also a member of a businessperson's luncheon club. Another member was bemoaning to Dan that he had entrusted his expensive Ducati racing bike to an apparently unreliable motorcycle repairman. The motorcycle mechanic was taking an exceedingly long time to make repairs, and the owner was becoming suspicious. Furthermore, the mechanic demanded payment before he delivered the bike. Then the supposed mechanic refused to tell the owner his bike's location. Dan laughed and told his friend that

Boyd & Associates could solve that problem for him. He said, "I'll bet you we can get your bike back." So Dan's friend took him up on the deal, and we took an imaginative approach to our investigation.

I knew the suspect lived in an apartment building in Sierra Madre, so we located his residence. Upon visiting the suspect's apartment building, we determined that no one would be allowed to repair motorcycles there. We suspected that the Ducati was probably being dismantled and sold for parts. Our first instinct was to check storage facilities near the mechanic's residence. We then researched storage lockers in the area.

We began calling, posing as the suspect mechanic, inquiring if the rent for storage was current. Private investigators are not under the same restrictions as police officers. While admittedly, in 2024, in order to gain information, one would have to give the last four of their Social Security number, their date of birth, and the name of their second-grade teacher. Back then, none was required. The storage facilities were more than happy to be helpful. The second one we contacted assured us that the rent was current. Jackpot. We explained we wanted to check on the storage locker but left the number at home, asking if he could provide it. He promptly replied, "237," and we were off and running.

The next day we rented a U-Haul trailer and went to the appropriate storage locker. The manager asked us to sign in, which we did—with the mechanic's name.

Using bolt cutters concealed under my partner's shirt, we made short work of the lock on unit 237, and lo and behold, there was the dismantled Ducati, along with another bike, which we ultimately left. We called the client, and he said to bring everything to him. Luckily, a large freight elevator was handy. In twenty minutes we loaded all the dismantled bike pieces into the U-Haul and relocked the storage unit with another lock we had prudently remembered to bring along. We drove immediately to the victim's home in Beverly Hills, where he assisted us in unloading his property.

I then mailed the key to the storage locker back to the supposed motorcycle mechanic. I wonder what went through his mind when he opened the door to the empty locker!

To say that our client was ecstatic would be an understatement. Our client was so happy he passed out generous bonuses to us. Dan Boyd also collected on his wager!

FAMILY MATTERS

By Patrick Boyd

HI, MY NAME'S PATRICK, and I am Ray's youngest son. I am going to tell a story from my perspective as the son of a criminal investigator.

When I was a kid, I knew my father to be one of the good guys. His job was to catch liars and cheaters. I am sure he had many sophisticated ways of catching criminals, but as a kid, the polygraph machine was the most memorable. The polygraph machine checked different bodily functions, including blood pressure, pulse, galvanic skin response, and the rate and amplitude of breathing.

When we were little, we called it "the box" because any time my dad wanted to know if we kids were lying, he would threaten to "put us on the box." (The threat was usually enough to make the guilty kid confess!)

To demonstrate the effectiveness of "the box," Dad would have us write down a number between one and ten on a piece of paper. We would put the paper in our pocket. Dad would then hook us up to "the box," and he would start by asking control questions. A control question is one where the only correct answer is no. For example, "Did you pick thirteen?" Because the only numbers were one to ten, obviously, thirteen was not one of the choices. The only answer was no.

"Did you pick fifteen?"

"No."

These control questions were meant to get the body settled and stable with "the box." Once settled, my dad would start with the real questions: "Did you pick ten? Nine? Eight?" and on down to "Did you pick one?" After he asked all ten possible numbers, my dad would examine the data and always pick the number that was written down in our pockets.

But my father also used to catch criminals by doing something called store shopping. Store shopping was an investigative trick in which one investigator would make a cash purchase while another would observe from a distance to see what the cashier would do with the money. I remember hearing stories about store shopping, but the first time I ever witnessed it was very exciting.

One of our neighbors owned the local car dealership. The dealership was experiencing some theft in the parts department, so they hired my dad to catch the thief. The owner identified the suspect as a kid in his early twenties with blond curly hair.

My dad got me in the car and told me we were going to the dealership to do some store shopping. When we walked into the dealership's parts department, I remember being very nervous as we stood off to the side while I looked bored, and my dad flipped through the pages of a parts book. I knew Dad had no idea what he was looking at since he had never worked on cars.

The young man behind the counter, who was clearly the suspect, approached and asked if he could help us. Dad politely said, "No, thank you." Just then, a man we'll call George, who worked for my father, came in the front door.

George went up to the counter and asked for a muffler for a 280ZX. The suspect left the counter and went to find that part in a box. The box was located where my dad and the owner had left it the night before, making it easy to find. When the clerk brought the box back to the counter, George slapped down $117 and some change on the counter. George said he was in a hurry and did not need a receipt. He picked up the 280ZX box and quickly went out the door.

I thought I would jump out of my shorts when I saw our suspect slide the money off the counter and put it in his pocket. My father quickly grabbed my hand and dragged me out the front door because he knew I wanted to start screaming, *"You thief! You thief!"*

My first store shopping was a success. The young man was later confronted and confessed to my dad. In his confession he admitted that he had stolen with a very easily accomplished system. He was the driver who delivered auto parts to body shops and car dealers. If they ordered six batteries, he would bring them eight and then pocket the money he received for the two extra batteries sold at a bargain price. My dad and the owner of the dealership prosecuted the employee. He was placed on six months probation and ordered to pay restitution as a condition.

STOLEN GOLF BALLS

By Patrick Boyd

BACK WHEN I was younger, I was a traveling professional golfer. I played on mini-tours and frequently traveled the country on the road. I traveled in a Ford Econoline van converted into a camper. Life was very fun on the road and a little different from how tour players may travel today. I think tour players who travel today fly NetJets from one town to another, and when they get to a new town, a volunteer hands them the key to a Mercedes. They then drive to the nicest resort in town, and when they get to the country club, there's a food buffet for them from six in the morning until three in the afternoon every single day. At the end of the week, the golf pros drive their Mercedes back to the private airport, give the key back to the volunteer, and get on their jet plane to travel to the next beautiful resort.

Back in the early '90s, I drove from town to town, playing on the Nike tour. It was sometimes a little bit difficult, but it was always a great adventure. One of the things I did to add to my revenue stream was to become a tour representative for the golf equipment company Maxfli. Most big companies had a corporate guy come from the office to give players golf balls, hats, and equipment, but Maxfli was a pretty small company, so they hired me, a player already on the tour, to take care of it for them.

I had between ten and twenty players every week, so Maxfli would just send the golf balls directly to a tournament site. On Monday afternoon I would go to the location at the event where the golf balls were stored, pick them up, and fill the players' lockers with golf balls, gloves, hats, and anything else that may have come for them. Any of the extra equipment I would just store in my van. There was a problem on tour with theft every single week. Representatives from all the different companies would complain that some of their products were stolen.

One week in Fort Smith, Arkansas, I had a case of Maxfli Revolution golf balls go missing. When I arrived on Monday to pick up the equipment, the gentleman behind the counter told me I had ten packages. After doing inventory, I realized I only had nine. With an entire case of golf balls (twelve dozen golf balls) missing, it would hurt my ability to give all the players the equipment they needed.

I complained to the man behind the counter about the missing box. He quickly informed me that he was the chief of police of Fort Smith, Arkansas, and he firmly believed that his security was so tight there was no way that those golf balls made it out of the locker room. He informed me that he had a security guard sitting at the desk until the locker room was closed and locked every evening. The police chief was just as upset about the loss of the golf balls as I was! He was convinced that those golf balls were still in the room because he said he himself checked in ten packages from UPS.

We devised a plan later that evening to check every single locker in the locker room and find out if the golf balls were there. I went and played nine holes in a practice round. When I came back, it was late in the afternoon and fairly quiet, so we decided to start our search. After searching several lockers, we came to the locker of a player named "Bud." In Bud's locker we found my case of Maxfli Revolution golf balls, which were suspiciously covered with a towel. It appeared that the box of balls had been hidden in the back of the locker. The police chief was furious. I needed those golf balls, so we took all the golf balls out of the box. Then we put the empty box back in the locker. The chief of police had a plan. The following day he was going to keep an eye on Bud's locker, and when he showed up in the morning, he would see how he reacted to seeing that box of Maxfli golf balls in his locker.

I went home that evening and couldn't sleep a wink because I was so excited to find out how those golf balls appeared in Bud's locker. When I showed up the next morning, the chief of police was very excited. He told me that Bud had shown up in the morning, opened his locker, suspiciously moved things around, checked over his shoulder, closed his locker, and then went to practice on the range. We immediately went to the tournament office to talk to the tournament coordinator from the PGA to see what we should do. They decided that we would go out onto the golf course, find Bud in his practice round, and have a discussion with him.

The chief of police, the tournament coordinator from the PGA Tour, and I got in a golf cart and drove out onto the golf course. We found Bud on the seventh green hitting practice putts. The tournament coordinator yelled out, "Hey, Bud, we need to talk to you for a second!" Bud looked very nervous, and although he said, "OK, I'll be there in a second," Bud proceeded to hit putts for several more minutes. I finally got frustrated and yelled, "Bud, get over here! We need to talk to you now!" Bud continued to shuffle around the putting green for a few seconds, had a few words with his caddy, and finally sauntered over to us at the back of the green where our cart was parked. After being confronted by the chief of police as to why the golf balls were in Bud's locker, Bud first claimed he had no knowledge of the golf balls whatsoever. When Bud was told he had been watched that morning, he realized we knew the golf balls were in his locker. He quickly came up with a story that he had been playing a practical joke on me.

Now I did not know Bud at all, and I had very little interaction with him in the past. We might have said hello to each other in passing, but we weren't close enough friends in any way, shape, or form where he could play practical jokes on me.

The PGA Tour decided they would suspend Bud from the tour for the next seven weeks, which I'm sure hurt him very much because he was on the money list and had a chance to keep his Tour Card for the following year. Bud decided to tell all the players that I was not a very good guy, and I didn't take the practical joke very well. Later, Bud wrote a statement to the PGA Tour, confessing that he had taken the balls because he was in financial trouble. Bud was planning to give the golf balls to his sponsor back at his country club as a thank-you for helping him out. It angered me that Bud had spread the word that I wasn't a very good guy. I had a copy of his confession sent to the Maxfli company. I also went to Kinko's, printed out a little letter of my own, and included the confession that Bud had written. I planned to make 150 copies and put one in every player's locker so that I could clear my name. The PGA Tour informed me that I would be in great trouble if I did that, but I thought clearing my name was more important. I went ahead and put an information packet stating that Bud was never to be trusted again, and my reputation was cleared.

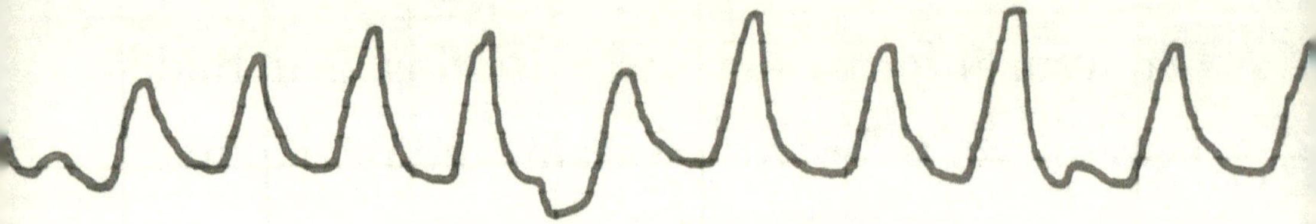

I'LL DRINK TO THAT!

By Patrick Boyd

A FEW YEARS LATER, I was still a tour professional and living in the Napa Valley. My wife (back then) worked in downtown Napa for a vineyard management business. She worked with a nice lady named Helen. Helen's husband, Ralph, worked at a local winery.

I had met Ralph before at a Christmas party. One day, out of the blue, he called me. He remembered that I told him my family did security, including criminal investigation. Ralph informed me that he suspected an employee in the tasting room of stealing and asked me if I had any suggestions. I was interested and excitedly told him I would meet him at 10:00 a.m. the following day at the winery across the street from his to discuss a plan. Later that evening I spoke with my dad, and we devised a plan to catch the thief.

The next morning I met Ralph at the winery near his. We stood at the bar as I explained my proposal.

I was to enter his winery's tasting room, posing as a customer. I would engage the suspect in friendly conversation, buy several bottles of wine, and leave when finished. We would then get the suspect out of the tasting room, and I would come back so we could figure out what the suspect had done with the money. Ralph knew six bottles of wine with tax would cost $154. I had enough cash to cover it, so I went to test our suspect. As I arrived, I noticed three people were exiting the tasting room. All three had six bottles in their hands and were headed for their car.

As I entered the tasting room, the suspect greeted me. "How are you?"

"I'm great and would very much like to do a wine tasting."

We talked about wine. I asked him, "If I pay cash, could I get a discount?" When the suspect said yes, I knew that was strike one—Ralph told me there was no discount for cash. At the end of the tasting, I proceeded to buy six bottles of wine, which I already knew would cost $154 after tax. I had the exact amount of money in my pocket. I marked the money with orange dots in the corners so I could trace the purchase.

When the suspect turned around to ring up the transaction, he did not use the cash register. He used a calculator. I knew that was strike two. When he turned back to me, the price he gave me for the wine was less than $154. The clerk was not smart enough to add in the tax, so I put $154 on the counter and another $20 for the tip (a common practice at Napa tasting rooms). I thanked him and went out the door.

I went across the street and called Ralph. I told him to get the suspect out of the tasting room, and I would then come back to the winery. Ralph and I went to the cash register and confirmed nothing had been rung up on the register the entire day. That meant the three people who were leaving when I entered the tasting room, each with six bottles in their hands, did not get rung up in the register either!

This was very quickly suspicious to us. Ralph took me to a vacant office while he called in our suspect.

When the suspect entered the office, I asked if he remembered me. He said, "Yes, you were a tasting room customer." My dad told me one of the things I had to do was scare our suspect, so at that point, I told him that I was a criminal investigator and that he was under arrest. I figured he was already a little nervous, so at this point, I told him to turn around and put his hands on the wall, and I was going to frisk him.

As the suspect complied, I remembered turning to Ralph, giving a little smile, and winking because I knew we had him already. As I frisked the suspect, I found a wad of cash in his sock underneath his pant leg.

I pulled the wad of money from his sock and placed it on a table. I spread it across the desk in front of me and could clearly see there was $154. The bright orange dots were in the corners of the bills I had placed there. There were also several other hundred dollar bills wrapped up in his sock. I figured the rest of that money had come from the customers at the tasting room before me.

I remember playing with the calculator on the desk while I asked the young man how long he had worked at the winery and how many hours a day he worked. I counted the money on the counter and did some calculations. I told the suspect, "Today, you have only been here for two hours, and you have stolen *X* amount of dollars. If you stole that amount every day for as long as you have worked here, the estimated amount you have stolen is $100,000!" It was over when the young man responded, "Oh no, I have not stolen *that* much money!"

At this point, I told the suspect he had to write out a confession. Based on my conversations with my father, I had the suspect start the confession with "I have been treated very respectfully and very politely by Mr. Boyd and

Mr. Ralph." He continued by writing that he was making his confession voluntarily. He then wrote that he had stolen $30,000 in cash. At the end of the confession, I told the suspect to write down that he gave me permission to search his home. He then signed and dated the confession.

I said, "Get up, let's go!"

"Where are we going?" he asked.

"We are going to your house to search." I thought he was going to cry.

When we got to the suspect's house, Ralph and the suspect stayed in the driveway. I went to the front door. The suspect's girlfriend answered, and I said, "I am a criminal investigator, and your boyfriend is under arrest. He gave me permission to search the house."

If she had been smart, she would have declined, but instead, she started to cry and let me inside. It was like Christmas morning! There were bottles of wine everywhere—three-liter bottles, five-liter bottles, etched bottles, wooden boxes, and cases of wine. There was so much wine that we had to get a refrigerated truck to come haul it all back to the winery.

Ralph was so mad, but ultimately, he decided not to prosecute. The decision not to prosecute was against my father's suggestion, but Ralph just wanted to fire the young man and get him out of the winery. I asked my dad why he was so intent on prosecuting the suspect. He explained that defense lawyers would counsel their clients, who had been fired from jobs for theft or any other misbehavior, to wait for one year until the statute of limitations for that particular offense had run and then sue for wrongful discharge. Ultimately, they would not prosecute.

CLOSER LOOKS AND HIDDEN CAMERAS

AS BOYD & ASSOCIATES continued to grow and evolve, we encountered a wide variety of cases that challenged us to think creatively and use new technologies. There were increasingly more times that employing innovative surveillance techniques helped us solve cases across different industries, as well as times that necessitated getting closer to customers—sometimes literally.

Perhaps you've heard the phrase, "What management inspects, employees respect." At Boyd

& Associates, we knew this to be true, and it was something we often shared with potential clients when we would occasionally have periods where it seemed we needed to advertise. We concentrated our efforts on corporations, emphasizing the need to pay attention to some of the most basic practices in their business operations. For example, every restaurant needs to religiously inspect every serial-numbered check and give special scrutiny to missing and voided checks. It's crucial to be aware of situations where the customer gets closer to your employee than top management can ever achieve.

I recall an investigation for a lumberyard that perfectly exemplifies this principle. A customer, a self-employed handyman, was building a patio for a homeowner. The handyman presented a crude drawing, and the salesman in the yard assisted in choosing the size and specifications for the lumber needed for the project. A few days later, the handyman again sought out the salesman he had consulted with on the earlier job. This time he wanted some door hardware and had brought along some cold beer in the cab of his truck.

Out of sight of the office, the two men chatted and drank. When it was time to write up the invoice, the salesman charged $60 when there should have been an $80 charge. Needless to say, the two men, emboldened by the success of their first adventure, had a mutually profitable summer.

We shopped the salesman, and after about three visits, he worked out a deal with our investigator, Dan Boyd, who conducted the interrogation and got a six-figure confession. As frustrating as it gets for the police when the district attorney refuses to prosecute on a case the police had worked to make an arrest, it was equally frustrating for us when the client said,

"My lawyer tells me not to prosecute. It's too much trouble."

While that case involved collusion between two men, an employee and a customer, it's important to remember that thieving is not confined to any particular group or gender—as you've already seen!

This became all the more clear when my own doctor brought me an intriguing problem. It seems that another doctor who practiced in the same building had confided in my provider that he thought his receptionist was stealing from him. He was averse to confronting her because she had become somewhat of a family friend, even babysitting for the doctor's wife.

Upon visiting the office, I noticed a light fixture over the reception desk where the suspect worked. The fixture contained three bulbs, and I immediately saw an opportunity. I explained to the victim doctor that if my crew could get into his office on the weekend, we could set up a hidden camera and review the receptionist's work later at our leisure. All of this made the doctor very nervous. I hesitated to remind him that it wasn't going to hurt a bit. (OK, I couldn't resist the opportunity!)

The Boyd alarm installation crew did an outstanding job with the hidden camera that next weekend. Sure enough, we got perfect results with the picture, and we watched Lisa, the receptionist, handle her job meticulously. The only break in the action was at noon when Lisa got up and went to lunch. Another girl, identified by the doctor as Margaret, slipped into her place.

She processed three people who were checking in for afternoon appointments. To the first two, she said, "That will be $20 for your copay." After collecting each copay, she bent down and reached for her purse, sliding the money from both patients inside. We later learned that the third patient had a policy that didn't require a copay, and yet Margaret had charged her $20, too.

A couple of days later, we went to the doctor's office and called Margaret in to look at the footage. She immediately started crying hysterically. We never could get an amount of theft from her, but we took her resignation and called it a day.

These cases demonstrate the importance of staying vigilant and thinking outside the box when it comes to investigating theft and fraud. Sometimes, the culprit isn't who you expect, and the methods for catching them require a bit of creativity and careful planning. Whether it's getting closer to customers to understand their interactions with employees or using innovative surveillance techniques, the key is to adapt our approach to each unique situation.

CONCLUSION: PERSONAL SECURITY

DURING THE 1990s the need for home and travel security was widely accepted. Boyd & Associates was proud to be at the forefront of the home security thrust. At one point we had over 1,100 uniformed security officers. We virtually guarded the majority of homeowner associations in the California desert environs. Gradually, we noted the improvement that the associations were making to secure their properties from both burglary and fire. Increasingly, our salespeople reported back to our offices with queries from our clients concerning closed-circuit television and other sophisticated security devices.

Advanced security thinking and planning were gradually swinging from manpower to devices. At Boyd & Associates, we responded by including specialized training to enable our workforce to be cognizant and comfortable with the new normal. The days with the retiree lugging the traditional watchman's clock on a prescribed route around the property to be protected were gone. Instead, we found that the basic security post required a trained computer operator, and no matter the remote location, the need for a weapon was obviated.

Interestingly, even when weapons in the hands of law enforcement came under fire, liberal thinkers demanded more use of such tactics after the murder of Michael Brown in Ferguson, Missouri.

One technique that had a surprising result was "stop and frisk," as employed by the New York City Police Department. Briefly, the technique depended on the initiation of the police on the street. Some have argued the technique depended on the intuition of the police on the street. Some have argued the technique should have been named "meet and greet" because gun-carrying citizens did not like the police officer on the street stopping them and requesting they submit to a search. The number of people carrying guns on the street dropped, as did the murder rate. President Obama and his attorney general did not like the result that countered their belief that the police department was the enemy of the Black race. Left-wing judges soon made stop and frisk an illegal technique. The murder rate went back up.

Even more difficulties faced law enforcement when vast groups began to demand police budgets be cut and even that the ranks of police be reduced. No bail arrests put the criminal back on the street almost before the arresting office had completed the paperwork. Left-wing prosecutors allegedly funded by George Soros managed to call every crime that resulted in the theft of less than $900 a misdemeanor. And certainly, crime ran rampant on America's streets.

Meanwhile, back at Boyd & Associates, the business kept growing. We sometimes felt like pallbearers at America's funeral. Dan Boyd countered with an almost prescient ability to acquire small alarm companies and seamlessly fold them into Boyd & Associates. The burglar alarm business is a lot more fruitful than the security guard business. While I met, employed, and still have many fine security guards at our company, there are some difficult problems associated with the manpower requirements.

California is a difficult location in which to employ people. The Division of Labor Law Enforcement is very antibusiness management. It is difficult to note that the average guard sergeant in charge of a location can get the company into a sexual harassment lawsuit merely by telling a female guard under his management that she looks nice in her uniform. Burglar alarms don't do that. Furthermore, the alarms don't smoke, drink, fail to show up for work, or sue the company for some imaginative grievance.

Greed is what fuels crime. It was the late J. Edgar Hoover who coined the truth statement: "Crime is a matter of greed, not need."

In 2013, Boyd & Associates sold the guard division with its 1,200 security guards and now focuses on burglar alarms, monitoring, and close-circuit television monitors. I am happily retired and living in the beautiful Napa

Valley. I enjoy attending church, spending time with my family, and watching baseball. (Go, Dodgers!) It was a good run, but I am happy to turn the reins over to Dan Boyd and let him manage for the next sixty years. Dan's early efforts at managing the company have been positively rewarding.

Left to right: Jack Boyd, President, Atlas Security; Kelly Boyd, Administrative Law Judge, State of California; Dan Boyd, President, Boyd & Associates; Patrick Boyd, retired golf professional

ABOUT THE AUTHOR

RAYMOND BOYD is a celebrated private investigator whose career spans decades of uncovering the truth behind some of the most intriguing and unusual cases. Known for his sharp wit and innovative approaches to solving crimes, Boyd has built a reputation not only for his skill in using polygraphs but also for his ability to connect with people on a personal level. Born and raised on the East Coast, Boyd's early years in the military and his stint as a stand-up comedian uniquely prepared him for a life of catching criminals and solving mysteries. After moving to California, Boyd established Boyd & Associates, a private investigation firm renowned for its effective investigative techniques and dedication to client service.

Boyd's first book, *God Bless Crime: It's Been Good to Me*, received praise for its humorous take on the serious business of crime-solving, and his second book, *Polygraphs and Paper Clip Bracelets*, continues in that tradition, offering readers more stories filled with clever crime-solving and laughter. Beyond his professional life, Boyd is a devoted father and grandfather who values family above all else. He often reflects on the balance between his demanding career and personal life, sharing wisdom and humor along the way.

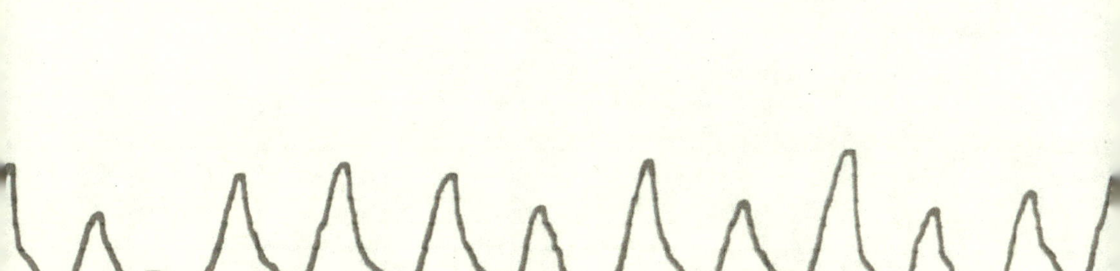

www.ingramcontent.com/pod-product-compliance
Lightning Source LLC
LaVergne TN
LVHW091548040926
847245LV00001B/7
* 9 7 9 8 8 9 1 8 8 1 2 9 7 *